Y0-BGD-993

UNTYING KNOTS

UNTYING KNOTS

TEN SIMPLE STEPS TO CONCLUDE A TOXIC RELATIONSHIP

JENNIE R. MARTIN

COPYRIGHT © 2008 BY JENNIE R. MARTIN.

ISBN: HARDCOVER   978-1-4363-2490-8
         SOFTCOVER   978-1-4363-2489-2

All rights reserved. No part of this book may be reproduced or transmitted in any form
or by any means, electronic or mechanical, including photocopying, recording, or by
any information storage and retrieval system, without permission in writing from the
copyright owner.

This book is intended to serve as a pocket reference. It is made to fit into pocket or purse
so it is handy for referral when needed.

The opinions expressed within this book are solely the opinions of the author. If you are on
medication you MUST consult your physician before discontinuing any prescriptions.

This book was printed in the United States of America.

To order additional copies of this book, contact:
Xlibris Corporation
1-888-795-4274
www.Xlibris.com
Orders@Xlibris.com
47664

CONTENTS

Dedicated to:

Those who are silent, and know better

INTRODUCTION

The inspiration for this book came from a dear friend who was upset and angry with her controlling husband. She related to me that she had gone out and bought some self help books and even left them out where he could see them! I was astonished that she felt that she ever had to hide her books, as in our home there are books of all types, many of which pertain to personal growth and self improvement.

When I related this story to another woman who had actually left an abusive husband, she was not a bit surprised. Apparently any attempt at empowering yourself is perceived as a threat to an abusive partner.

Thus the title: UNTYING KNOTS. The cover looks like a scout handbook and sounds like one as well. It appears completely non-threatening. The real knots you untie, of course, are the knots that keep you tied up in a negative relationship.

You may untie these knots and find yourself able to leave the relationship and create a new positive environment for yourself. You may be able to stay and get your partner and yourself help and work things out. Either way, you will have a better quality of life.

If you have children, I urge you to create a happy and stress-free home for them. You must break the cycle of abuse. The world can be changed, one family at a time.

My wish for you is that every morning you wake up in joy and every evening you sleep in peace.

Love and blessings,

Jennie R. Martin

CHAPTER ONE

BECOMING AWARE

Day after day articles appear in newspapers and magazines describing how to tell if one's partner is an abuser. These articles abound with the signs to look for and the questions to answer. I believe that if you are in a controlling or abusive relationship you already know the answer to those questions.

If you are being used, abused or mistreated in any way, chances are good that you know about it. Most certainly someone has pointed it out to you more than once. What you do not have is awareness. AWARE, according to the World Book Dictionary-having perception or knowledge; conscious, informed.

Listen to what you are saying when you speak, become conscious of what is going on in your life. When your friends invite you out is it an invitation minus your partner? Are you allowed to go out with your friends at all? These are all clues! Controllers and abusers usually start a relationship by slowly isolating the object of their affection from their family and friends. It is generally done under the guise of "loving you so much" or "I need to be with you all the time." They actually do not want anyone other than themselves to be influential or supportive. Next they will try to undermine the self esteem with subtle put downs. Of course, these tactics increase in intensity the longer the relationship lasts.

The point is, never settle for less than what is right and good for you. Everyone deserves a peaceful life, enough food, a hot shower and a warm clean bed. Home should always be a haven for the people residing there, a place to be happy to return to at the end of the day.

If you are on any of the popular medications for anxiety or depression, you are merely masking the symptoms of the source of your pain. It's sort of like saying, "Gee, my leg is broken but I can walk on it just fine while my morphine is working!" Just as physical pain is a symptom of some malady in the physical body, emotional pain is indicative of something not going right in the emotional part of our being.

When something or someone causes you enough emotional pain to have you running for tranquilizers, you need to evaluate the situation. If life is uncomfortable or painful, it is a sign that something needs to change, and YOU, and only you can change it. Yes, there are people who need medications for bona fide mental health issues, but I have a strong notion that a huge percentage of the prescriptions written for stress and depression are unnecessary and ultimately harmful.

If you place your hand upon a hot stove and it hurts, do you go to the doctor and ask him for pills so that the next time you put your hand on that hot stove you won't feel it? That is absurd, is it not? You would never go back to a doctor who would consider something like that!

Your emotional health is compromised when you do not address what is causing the stress and it is allowed to continue, just as the skin and flesh of your hand would be permanently disfigured if you repeatedly burned yourself.

If I can feel the pain I can find it and I can fix it. If nothing can be felt, nothing can be fixed.

God, or whomever you consider your Supreme Being, can heal any wound whether it is physical, emotional, psychological or spiritual. Choose healing, ask and you shall receive. You must remember, however, God helps those who help themselves. It may take time and a good deal of daily work on yourself, but as you get stronger you will see that the result is worth it.

Sometimes people who tolerate abuse from others are, in turn, abusive to those who are somewhat weaker than they are; for instance their children or pets. If you are an abuser there is no way that you don't know about it. You know you are out of control, get help immediately. Asking for help is nothing to be ashamed of.

You must also decide if it is help you want or just sympathy. Do you like to take time and energy from others by complaining? We all need to talk things out, but at some point the talking has to end and there has to be some action.

* Your first step: Become aware of your circumstances and look at your situation with honesty.

CHAPTER TWO

RISING CONSCIOUSNESS

When there is dysfunction in a family (I use this word for lack of a better term, I think it is sorely overused.) it is worse than a fast spreading cancer. It affects all members of the family and filters outward even to friends and co-workers.

Now that you have faced yourself and admitted that there is a problem, you will invariably notice many more injustices all around you. Just like the psychological system where, for instance, you buy a new car and all of a sudden everywhere you go you see numerous cars of the same make and model, you will see things like never before.

Noticing so many injustices at once can be terribly overwhelming. You cannot possibly deal with all of them at once. Draw in a few deep breaths and hold on, you are ready to take command of your situation. Remaining calm is essential, it is also powerful.

*   Now that you are tired of being a doormat, it is time to get up off the floor!

You do not have to accept what you assume life has handed you. Set goals for yourself, decide what it is that YOU want and go after it! You have the power of choice. For example:

Junk food or ——————————— healthy food

Exercise or——————————— flipping TV channels aimlessly

Drugs and excessive alcohol or——— lots of pure water

Helping or ——————————— hurting

Burying you head in the sand or——— facing your situation head on

Become as healthy as you can, fear takes over when the body is depleted and fatigued. Why do you think that in concentration camps people were starved and worked to the point of exhaustion? The prisoners were easy to control in that condition.

The most loving thing you can do for your family and friends is to become the strongest person you can be. Then you can stand on your own and no one has to fix you, bail you out of a jam or listen to you complain.

That is not to say that you have to be a mean sort, rather the opposite. A strong person knows how to say no effectively. A strong person can also make a firm point without losing his or her cool. A tough person is not necessarily a strong person.

* If every one of us just took care of our own little part of the world, there would be little need for programs of assistance.

There are also many mixed up people who, for whatever reason, think that by "helping others" they can dismiss the mess they are in. How can you possibly fix anyone in any way, especially if you cannot begin to help yourself? Start right where you are, fix yourself and all will fall into place. Make yourself respectable and respect yourself! People mirror your own thoughts about yourself.

* If you treat yourself with respect, people are likely to follow suit.

Look around you and notice the relationship dynamics wherever you go. Start a study of human beings; it is fun and informative! Look for the exchanges of energy and try to figure out the causes and effects of these exchanges.

It can also be a big help with your own relationships if you take a third party approach and see it as if you are a bystander with no emotional attachment.

When you are not experiencing success in your relationships try to change your approach. As the old saying goes, if you keep doing what you are doing you will keep getting what you are getting! Change your approach as many times as it takes to make a positive change in your situation.

God made the good stuff for his children. Where did the idea come from that God does not want us enjoying the life he so graciously gave us?

*   Your second step: Raise your consciousness and see that you can change your life into what you always dreamed it could be.

CHAPTER THREE

SETTING THE GROUND RULES

First and most importantly, you are doing yourself and others a great disservice when you tolerate abusive and controlling behavior from anyone!

If all the abused got fed up on the same day and stopped tolerating the abuse, then all the abusers would have no choice but to change their behavior and come up with a different approach to their human relations.

Do you think that people who are interested in being in control are going to go looking for someone like themselves? Not on your life! They will look for someone who appears easy to control. When you make yourself a victim it is almost as if the abusers and controllers can pick you out. You may as well be wearing a sign that says "USE ME."

Once you can muster up the courage to proclaim, even silently, that you are no longer willing to be mistreated, your presentation of yourself will improve. Again, you do not have to be a mean, surly person so that people will not walk on you. If your body language sends out the signals that you are strong and self-assured, others are less likely to attempt to take advantage of you.

You have to follow with action, decide where to draw the line and train yourself to make it clear that you have zero tolerance with unacceptable behavior. When it comes to abuse, there will be no second chances. Ideally, there will not be a first chance.

In chapter seven we will address several ways that can help you to look and feel better thus providing a better self image. The better you look, the better you feel, the better you act and treat others and yourself, and the more self confidence you exude.

When it comes to children, I have a few opinions. Agree or disagree it is what I believe would be best for the children.

First, I believe we need to limit the amount of children we bring into the world. You need to know your levels of tolerance. True, there have been many successful large families, but not without sacrifice. It takes a tremendous amount of work, time, patience and love to nurture a sizeable family. If you are limited on patience or time and especially love, keep your family small. There is little excuse with today's modern medicine to become pregnant by accident. Each child deserves a great deal of his parent's attention, especially during the early years. If your patience level is low, stop at one, two at the most and spread them out.

Money also has to be a consideration. Children are an expense and you want to be able to train and educate them properly. Your goal for your children is to prepare them to go off into the world as well adjusted adults and self-supporting citizens.

Again, children definitely require a large investment of your time; this is very important.

* PRIORITY: Do not ever choose a favorite. Sure, some kids are easy going and some can be difficult, they are people! Find the greatness in each and enjoy! They are young for such a short time.

In addition, children need discipline and I am not talking about beating them! Many of you who are reading this book have been abused as children. If you have been abused it is extremely important that you DO NOT STRIKE YOUR CHILD. The tendency to lose control is too prevalent. There are a number of good parenting books available with some great techniques to help you with discipline. My favorite authors of books of this type are Dr. Kevin Leman and Dr. Spencer Johnson. Anything by these two men is invaluable in raising well-adjusted children.

Think about it, no one likes to be in the company of unruly children. Badly behaved children will have a hard time making and keeping friends, even the grandparents cringe when they see the little darlings coming! You are not doing your children any favors by letting them run wild. You are actually harming them, many times for life, because they will grow up lacking the skills necessary to be successful adults.

Another way to harm your children is by allowing yourself to continue to be a victim. Children learn by example and they will either end up emulating your behavior or the behavior of the abuser.

You do not want to raise doormats and you do not want to raise abusers. Period.

Get out a pencil and paper and write down what you will accept in your relationships and what you will not accept. Read this several times a day. These will be your new rules to live by. Let them sink deep into your subconscious mind so that you know without thinking about it what you will tolerate and what you will not.

*   Your third step: Set the ground rules, it really is alright to rock the boat.

CHAPTER FOUR

ESTABLISHING A GAME PLAN

In creating your game plan, it is necessary to sit down with a pencil and lots of paper and first write down what you have to gain and what you have to lose by changing your situation.

After you have these gains and losses written in the proper columns, decide what is tolerable in your situation and what absolutely must go. Because it is often easier to fight the small battles, there are actually people who can tolerate an unfaithful spouse but will not tolerate a pair of dirty socks lying around. Personally, I'd rather see the socks of a kind and faithful spouse on the floor next to the hamper!

Change can be frightening to some people and it is important to visualize your goals, actually seeing the end result in your mind's eye. Make a habit of seeing your perfect life in your mind for five minutes each day; it will make a big difference.

Several years ago Bill Murray and Richard Dreyfus starred in a movie titled "WHAT ABOUT BOB." It was a comedy about a psychiatrist and his patient, Bob. The premise of Bob becoming sane was based on his taking "baby steps" toward that goal. This is actually a valid technique! Start small and work your way up to being the person you want to be, more assertive and decisive.

If, for instance, you have a difficult time saying no, try saying no to a telemarketer. There are certainly enough telephone solicitations to do that! After you master that, go to a car lot and practice there. You will find many opportunities each day to say no.

Reward yourself when you have done something that helps to empower you. Get your hair done, buy a new lipstick or a special treat for yourself.

* Something important to keep in mind when you are deciding what is tolerable:

* You must always strive to make your home a haven for all who reside there. There are so many battlegrounds outside your doors, there is no reason to subject your family to one at home. No one should ever dread coming home; home needs to be a good place to be.

* Unconditional love is the only healing force in the Universe. This means that you have to love yourself unconditionally and respect yourself enough to expect loving relationships.

I often reflect on Jesus' words to the cripple, "Stand up and walk." My interpretation of this is "get up off your anatomy and do something to help yourself."

****ACTION BEGINS WITH A DECISION.

When you decide that you are going to make a serious change in your life, focus on how good your situation can be instead of the perceived fear of change. Change is your friend; you will be changing and growing all through your life. Facing change, however, is often more frightening to some people than the abuse, neglect and disrespect they live with each and every day. Decide finally that you are going to make the beautiful life that each human on Earth deserves.

Creating that beautiful life for you and your children is much more positive than focusing on revenge. When you keep score, everyone loses. Revenge is poison, let it go. The sweetest revenge anyone can have is creating a beautiful, successful life.

*   This is also a good time to create your exit strategy. An exit strategy is essential whether you are in a bad situation or not. Consider opening your own personal bank account and start saving whatever you can off to the side for an emergency.

Talk to someone you know you can trust about your situation so that someone is at least aware of your circumstances. You may need a safe haven someday and you need someone to help you get there.

Often people are ashamed to tell others about the abuse they suffer. You have nothing to be ashamed about! The abusers are the ones that should be ashamed, but they may try to make you fearful to tell anyone what is happening. Do not be afraid anymore. There is help available and those who love you are waiting to hear that you are changing your situation.

You will probably need a lawyer sooner or later. Get good referrals on this especially if you need to protect your children. If you don't presently have a job, you will need to find one and/or take classes to make yourself more marketable. Look into victims resources in your area; you will be surprised at how much help is available.

Many times people fear leaving a bad situation because they can't stand the thought of being by themselves.

Get comfortable with yourself, learn to enjoy your own company, it's good to be able to spend alone time. Practice by having lunch alone in a restaurant or going to a coffee shop alone. Taking classes is very positive also whether it is for future employment or just personal growth. You may find that you enjoy your own company!

*   Your fourth step: Establish your game plan, because if you want to build a beautiful home, you will need a blueprint.

CHAPTER FIVE

DECISIONS, DECISIONS

It is such an incredibly easy task. Your friend needs to make a decision. It is very simple for outsiders to see what should be done, what is best. An outsider will see the circumstances from a different perspective and, with little or no emotional attachment to the situation, will wonder why there is a decision to be made at all.

Making a decision for ourselves however, can be stressful. When the outcome is not clear to us we can become paralyzed within the decision making process.

*   A decision is simply, choosing a path.

It is perfectly all right to ask for advice from people you respect regarding your decisions. Make sure you are talking to people who you would model your life after. For instance, if your spouse is physically abusive, do not ask another victim of abuse what they would do. You can clearly see what they are doing! Talk to someone who has successfully cut the ties to an abusive spouse.

Ideally, you will seek the advice of a professional counselor trained to deal with people in your situation. In addition, advice can be good, but you are ultimately responsible for what happens to you and your minor children.

*   Never relinquish control of your life to anyone else . . . . EVER!

*   An important step to remember: Stuff happens in our lives.

NO ONE IS IMMUNE TO ANYTHING.

NO ONE LIVES A CHARMED LIFE.

A very good exercise is to go over in your mind, or on paper, different scenarios that could possibly happen to you. I am not saying to start worrying about all the things that can go wrong in your life. I am asking you to come up with game plans in the event that you hit a bump in the road. For example, while you are gainfully employed it is good to think of what steps you would take if you lost your job. What steps would you take if you were told you had a grave illness? It is important to have an outline of options when things are going well and you are healthy. If you are then faced with setbacks, at least you can put yourself on autopilot for awhile until you can re-group and think clearly.

Face these possibilities as just what they are, only possibilities that may never occur. At least you will know what preliminary action to take should there be a need.

As far as relationship decisions:

*   Decide what you want.

*   Write down what you want.

*   Visualize daily what your ideal life will be like.

*   Settle for no less.

*   Your fifth step: Make your decisions with care, if you do not, others will be happy to decide for you.

CHAPTER SIX

ENFORCING
THE GROUND RULES

Enforcing the ground rules: Many people can talk the talk, but when it comes to walking the walk, well that is when things fall apart.

What is the solution? Practice comes to mind. Now that you have established what your rules are, it is only a matter of processing whether they are being followed. The main problem here is that some of us bend the rules readily depending on the day or the mood or . . . . this is not good. If something is not to be tolerated, it must not matter what day of the week it is. Keep on track and practice discipline.

Disciplined people are happy people. They are more successful, more prosperous, healthier and happier mostly because they can be more creative. They do not have to think about what is right or what is the easy way out.

Enforcing the ground rules also means standing up to the bully. The bully can be in the disguise of a wife, husband, Mom, Dad, boyfriend, girlfriend or child. Yes, a child can bully a parent; usually this is learned by example. If a parent is weak, there is no one for the child to look to for strength.

Abuse, of course, does not always mean physical abuse. Unfortunately it is only one avenue and it leaves the physical scars. The emotional scars can be worse, enough to bring a big man to tears decades after the fact.

Once everyone involved your life knows that you will no longer be wishy-washy, acceptance will occur and the challenges will be fewer until the habit is broken.

* Important: About standing up to the bully, if you are in a dangerous situation, GET OUT NOW! If you read the newspaper you cannot help but notice that entire families are being murdered by abusers. Run and do not look back, there are people who can help you.

Do not be embarrassed about asking for help, that is not a sign of weakness. Just because a tree bends in a storm does not mean that it is weak!

Many times people who allow themselves to be victims say that they just don't want to hurt anyone. I have news for you, the abuser does not care who he hurts, especially you and possibly your children. It is understandable that you may feel sorry for the abuser because, of course, he/she is almost always the product of abuse. That is why you have to take action! Abuse is a cycle that has to be broken.

***Remember, when you force an abuser to seek help, you are helping them to get well. If no one insists, these people will rarely seek help on their own. With the proper counseling they can enjoy life more because their relationships will be richer and more loving.

Bottom line, you do not have to tolerate abuse so DON'T! You are the only one who can stop the abuse.

* Do not blame God and beg Him to change your lot in life. God can only work with you if you give Him something to work with. Do not blame God or use Him as a scare tactic on your family. He gets enough of a bad rap as it is. God has never been out to "get" anyone except to love them.

* The laws of the universe are set. If you break the laws you pay the consequences. God is not on guard duty. Help yourself as best you can and trust Him for what you cannot do.

* Your sixth step: Enforce the ground rules; you will like yourself better when you are consistent.

CHAPTER SEVEN

LOOKING GOOD
AND FEELING GREAT

Does it not seem that when you go out and you do not feel you look your best, you do not have the best day possible? However, when you are in THAT outfit, your hair is behaving, and your face is looking good, you feel like you can take on the world!

Did you ever notice that many times when a person wants to exercise control over another, they discourage any effort that could improve that person's appearance?

This is a ploy to keep the victim's self esteem in the gutter. Remember, the better you look, the better you feel, the better you feel, the better you treat others, the better you treat others, the better they treat you and on and on and on.

* Someone who truly cares for you wants you to look good and feel good about yourself and is proud to be with you. This applies, of course, to men as well as women.

Children should be taught good grooming from early childhood. Good habits always serve us. No one wants to be the icky, smelly kid in class, how humiliating! This leaves permanent emotional scars. Please teach your children to be proud of themselves and take care of their appearance.

Keep your face and body clean. Keep your teeth clean and your breath fresh. Exercise and take some vitamins. As you feel better about yourself it will show from the inside out. Strength equals power. Good grooming does not require a great deal of cash. Your self-confidence will expand greatly when you are looking and feeling good.

Appearance is one vital key but if when you open your mouth you undo everything, forget about it! WATCH YOUR POTTY MOUTH! It is never cool, sophisticated or powerful to use words that need to be beeped out! It is unnecessary and crude. Never use foul language in front of children, EVER! Learn some positive words or keep your mouth shut.

Earn your keep; give your employer an honest day's work for an honest day's wage. The pride and confidence that comes from a job well done always makes a person more attractive.

* If your job is to stay home and take care of children, know that you hold the future of the Earth in your hands.

Make a good home wherever you are planted. Do your work with pride and you will create the mental muscle to succeed. You will then be someone who can feel great about being you!

* In the interest of future relationships, if you want to attract a winner, you must BE a winner!

* Your seventh step: Look and feel great. You owe it to yourself!

CHAPTER EIGHT

THE GOLDEN RULE

No one knows what a kind word or action can and will do for another person. Treat others as you would like to be treated. Simply put, this is what the Golden Rule says. (Of course, if you enjoy abuse, strike that last thought!)

Listen to yourself very carefully for the next few weeks. How would you like to have yourself as a Mom, Dad, spouse, co-worker, etc.? Be honest.

Humans are creatures of habit, going through most of their days on autopilot. One of the most dangerous aspects of this fact is that many of us have created a litany of negative statements that we incant regularly. Change that habit by changing your self-talk. When you regularly speak in a positive way to yourself AND others, it brightens everyone's day.

Always be truthful. Lying is complex and disrespectful to others as well as it is to you. That is not to say that you should tell Aunt Gertie that her dress is ghastly. You know what I mean! Be yourself in your relationships, no lies either verbal or assumed.

Never cheat on your mate, it is probably one of the most devastating and disrespectful acts that anyone can do. The partner that cheats can almost never win back any trust and the person he/she cheated with can certainly not be trusted. So, you ladies and gentlemen who have a beau on the side, if you make the break with your spouse are you going to trust the next one? The other woman/man was cheating with a married person. Think about it.

When entering a new relationship, if you EVER have the thought that you can "change" your new love interest, walk away at once! People are responsible for their own growth and change. There are companions out there who are already compatible with you. Do not settle for less than you want just because you dislike being alone.

Earn your keep, don't be a taker. Pull your weight on the job as well as around the house. Take pride in your home. Even on a limited income you can be neat and clean about yourself and your home. Many times a limited income is the father of creativity!

Use clean language wherever you go and especially at home. We all know people who only seem to know one or two adjectives. This is a sign of ignorance. Yes, we have freedom of speech but it's also other people's right not to hear trashy talk.

*** Especially be mindful of how you speak to and interact with your children. Their little minds are soaking up everything. Be positive when explaining things to children. Always let them know they are loved. The human mind is the most powerful computer ever; it will process negative input as well as positive without discrimination.

Always speak of your family in a positive way to others. Sometimes make sure they can hear you! People will behave the way you expect them to behave, so expect your children to be winners. Everyone really wants to be a winner!

* Your eighth step: Discover the power of your words and actions. You will be pleasantly surprised at the response you will receive.

CHAPTER NINE

GAINING MOMENTUM

By slowly changing your outlook as well as your habits, you will begin to feel stronger and more self-confident. You are really building some mental muscle now. No one can build this for you; it simply does not work that way. The same way no one can exercise for you and build physical muscle. You are the one who has to work out!

You must become the emotionally strongest person that you can possibly be. If you can't take care of yourself you can't possibly take care of someone else. You will be too weak and that is a state that you will not return to ever again.

If you live in fear of someone and you are, in fact, in danger, it is time to get out. Run and do not look back. This is not a cowardly act. The abusers are the cowards in this world.

When it comes to matters of addiction in your family, whether it is drugs, alcohol, gambling, etc. you must be prepared to walk away. Most addicts will not seek help until they hit bottom and that will not happen while someone is taking the heat for their addictive behavior. Many times the only loving thing that can be done for an addict is to let them go. This is usually the only option when their behavior is harming children.

*** If you do nothing to protect your children from the effects of abuse you are equally as guilty as the one who is actually abusing them. Psychologically, it is my belief that it is as difficult for children, once grown up, to forgive the parent who stood by and did nothing, as it is to forgive the abuser.

Being truthful is of the utmost importance. Especially do not lie to yourself! Lying is much too difficult anyway. It takes entirely too much energy to keep track of all the tales that have been told, not to mention the energy it steals from the liar as well as the one being lied to.

If you lie to someone more than twice, it is unlikely that you will be believable thereafter.

Stand by your principles, have the courage of your convictions. Others do not have to agree with you. You are the only person who knows what is right for you. Today do something brave, for your own sake. You will have to get used to calling the shots when you move on. For some, it is easier and more comfortable to have someone telling them what to do and when to do it. This is not you anymore.

Just to prove to yourself that you have what it takes, face one of your fears today! If you are afraid of bugs, go to the pet store and look closely at the big spiders. If you are afraid of talking to other people, go to the pharmacy and ask someone to explain aspirin. You'll learn something! Better yet, go to the rest home and talk to a resident about the old days. You may find a new, good friend there.

Each and every morning it is good to start out by reading something positive. There are countless authors of uplifting books and articles to choose from. Nourishing your soul is something that should be done daily, like exercise for your body.

*** The mental muscle that you create is going to be there when you need it, just as the physical muscle is there when called upon.

Mostly, please do not give up on yourself. You have spent a lifetime with you, and would be setting yourself up for disappointment to expect everything to be better overnight. Take it a step at a time and you will be surprised how permanent the changes will become.

* Your ninth step: Keep visualizing the goal. You have to see it first to believe it!

CHAPTER TEN

FLY!

You are probably asking yourself, "Where do I go if I do leave this situation? I can't go back to good old Mom." This can be tough. If your situation is dangerous you may have to go back to Mom and Dad for awhile. If necessary, there are shelters that can be located through churches and social services. If you do have time to prepare, you need to start saving money off to the side to use as a security deposit and first month's rent.

Much of the problem with leaving, however, is pride. We are so afraid of what others will think of us that we sacrifice our own happiness and safety. We are afraid of appearing as a failure and we are afraid of embarrassing our family. Stop right here. Other people think less about us than we think. They are busy with their own lives! Fear will immobilize you if you dwell on it. Look ahead to your good future.

This book is written for those who truly desire to change their situation. In the afterword, there are interviews with people that I know very well.

These individuals have left abusive situations and have gone on to find healthy relationships. Perhaps their stories will help you see that it can be done and a new, beautiful life is possible.

Remember, only you can live your life, no one else has been given that privilege. Change your thoughts and you can begin to experience changes in your situation.

*** NO ONE DESERVES TO BE ABUSED! DO NOT TAKE IT AND ABSOLUTELY DO NOT GIVE IT OUT!

If children are involved, decide to always put their welfare before all else; you will be richly rewarded with a beautiful legacy.

As a review:

1. Become conscious of the problems in your relationships.

2. Become aware that you are the only one capable of changing your situation.

3. Start out by setting up your rules for living. Do not try to tolerate the intolerable.

4. Enforce your rules with others as well as yourself!

5. Always look to what you are gaining, not losing.

6. Establish your game plan, baby steps if necessary.

7. Look good every day, practice self discipline.

8. The golden rule. Life is NOT a sitcom.

9. Gain strength, work mental and physical muscles.

10. Enjoy the beautiful life you have created.

Abuse does not just affect you. It, of course, affects your children. It also affects your unborn children. It affects everyone who has an association with you. It affects the next generation and the next and the next.

Someone, please say stop.

Two women who successfully broke free of controlling, abusive spouses share their stories:

A female in her twenty's

1. What was the initial attraction?
   a. He was fun!

2. When did you notice that there was a control issue?
   a. When he started telling me who I could hang out with and telling me I couldn't cut my hair.

3. How soon after you got together did the abuse start?
   a. The controlling behavior started about 6 to 8 months into the relationship. There was never any physical abuse toward me, mostly name calling after we were married. This was 3 ½ years after we started seeing each other. He did beat my dog and eventually shot him (the dog.)

4. When your family reacted or said something about the relationship, did you think about what they said or did you shut them out?
   a. They hated him and that's all I ever heard. I think it pushed me toward him.

5. What specific behaviors made you frightened or uncomfortable?
   a. I was never afraid of him, I could have kicked his a**!

6. What steps did you take to get started out of the relationship?

    a. It wasn't steps. I just decided one day that I was done and when I make up my mind to do something there is no changing it.

7. What is your level of education?

    a. High school diploma and Cosmetology school.

8. What would you like to share with a person in a similar situation?

    a. There's always something better, you can't settle for what isn't good for you. My aunt gave me the best advice. She told me "If you were in prison for ten years and they said you could leave tomorrow, would you stay because you were used to it?"

9. What advice would you give family and friends of others in your former situation?

    a. You may think you should keep quiet about the situation, but you shouldn't. The person suffering may be upset at you when you point out traits of abuse, but they know you are right. Just be there for support and try not to judge. They'll eventually "get it."

10. Did you go to family and friends for help? Why or why not?

    a. I generally don't ask for help. I talked to family and friends but I already knew what I wanted to do.

11. Are you happy today, and why?

    a. Very, I have the absolute best and most perfect, understanding, trusting and not the least bit controlling husband and two beautiful children. My husband is just as good a father as he is a husband.

A female in her forties

1. What was the initial attraction to this person?

    a. The initial attraction was a common interest in doing fun things, like flying or going on cruises.

2. When did you notice that there was a control issue?

    a. The day we got married. We had a long distance "courtship" so weekends together were always fun, not real life.

3. How soon after you got together did the abuse start?

    a. Mental, within a few years. Subtle mental, perhaps immediate but I didn't recognize it until I looked back and re-examined the relationship.

4. When your family reacted or said something about the relationship, did you think about it or did you shut them out?

    a. I never said a word to my family until the day I left.

5. What specific behaviors made you frightened or uncomfortable?

    a. Failure, it was my fault that I couldn't make it work.

6. What steps did you take to get started out of the relationship?

    a. I worked overtime and saved money on the side. I had always turned my whole check over to him.

7. What is your level of education?

    a. Masters degree

8. What would you like to share with another person in a similar situation?

    a. It doesn't ever get better by "waiting to see if it will." It always escalates and gets worse. Also, tell your family as it happens, you need support, not isolation.

9. What advice would you give family and friends of others in your former situation?

    a. If you know something (like a partner is cheating) then speak up! And, family should always support their own, not side with the ex!

10. Did you go to family and friends for help? Why or why not?

    a. My sisters are my strength. Still I did not tell them until I was ready.

11. Are you happy today and why?

    a. I married a wonderful man and we are great friends. Wait until this happens, don't settle. I also took control of my life. I don't tolerate rude or mean people ever and I eliminate as much stress from my life as possible, this includes stressful people!

10009121R0

Made in the USA
Lexington, KY
16 June 2011